The 1960s

Ariel Books

Andrews and McMeel
Kansas City

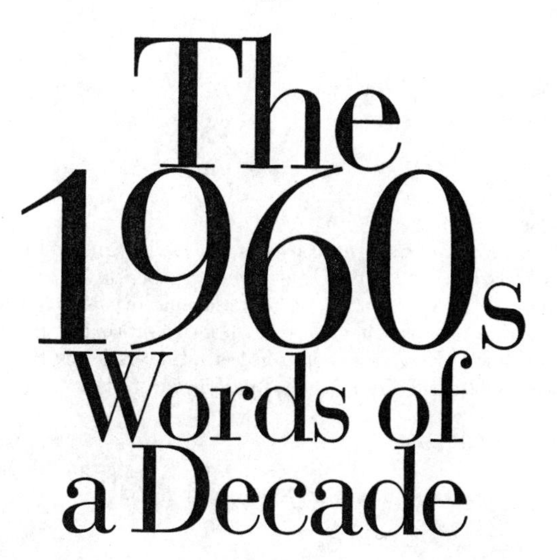

The 1960s Words of a Decade

For information write Andrews and McMeel, a Universal Press Syndicate Company, 4900 Main Street, Kansas City, Missouri 64112.

ISBN: 0-8362-0713-0

Library of Congress Catalog Card Number: 95-76433

Contents

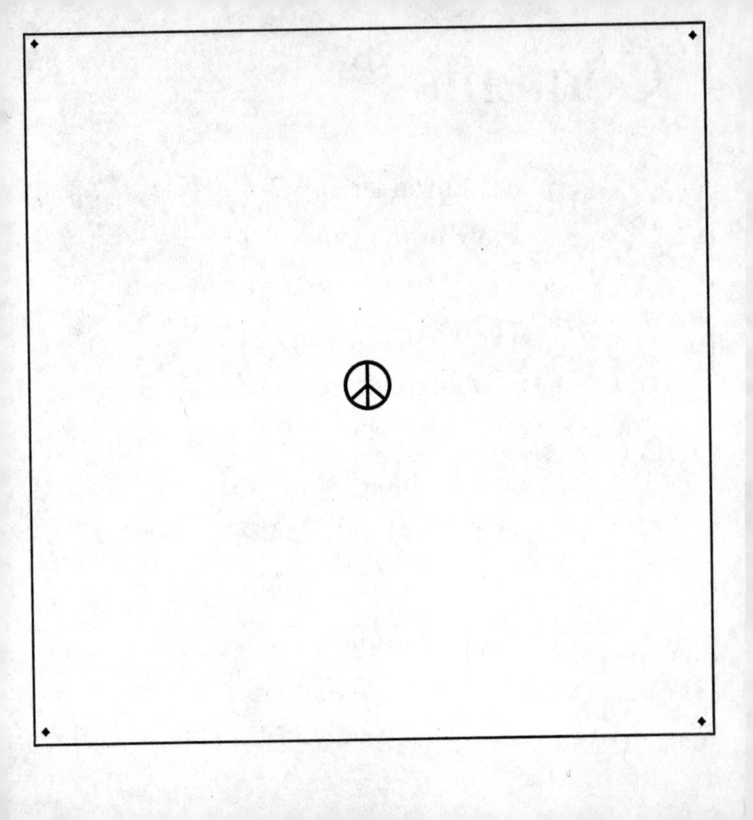

Introduction

We stand today on the edge of a new frontier—the frontier of the 1960s—a frontier of unknown opportunities and perils—a frontier of unfulfilled hopes and threats.

JOHN F. KENNEDY
thirty-fifth president of the United States

This riveting collection of quotations will take you back to an era of hope, liberation, and togetherness, but also one of turmoil, despair, and social

upheaval. John F. Kennedy, Martin Luther King, Jr., Betty Friedan, Richard M. Nixon, Mick Jagger, Janis Joplin, and Andy Warhol are just a few of the fascinating personalities quoted in this wide-ranging survey of a decade.

Public sentiment swung wildly back and forth between exhilaration and despondency during the sixties. From the tragedies of the Vietnam War and political assassinations to the glories of space exploration and the successes of the civil rights and women's liberation movements, Americans weathered one shock after another. Emotional highs and lows were further kindled by the cultural shifts of the time: the explosion of rock music, a widening

generation gap, the nuclear threat, innovations in art and fashion, and the counterculture movement.

The sixties were a unique time in American history and one that will live on in our memories. Despite the outward confusion and complexity of the times, there was often a sense of uniformity and coming together to face the larger issues. As Myrlie Evers, widow of the slain civil rights activist Medgar Evers nostalgically reflects, "I miss what we had during that time . . . a sense of purpose, people coming together, meeting the challenges head-on, a kind of solidarity you don't find anymore."

State of the Union

Washington is a city of southern efficiency and northern charm.

—John F. Kennedy
thirty-fifth president of the United States

The real 1960s began on the afternoon of November 22, 1963 . . . It came to seem that Kennedy's murder opened some malign trap door in American culture, and the wild bats flapped out.

—Lance Morrow

writer

And so, my fellow Americans, ask not what your country can do for you; ask what you can do for your country. My fellow citizens of the world, ask not what America will do for you, but what together we can do for the freedom of man.

—John F. Kennedy

thirty-fifth president of the United States

We're eyeball to eyeball, and I think the other fellow just blinked.

—Dean Rusk

U.S. secretary of state, on the Cuban missile crisis

None of us here in Washington knows all or even half of the answers. You people out there in the fifty states had better understand that. If you love your country, don't depend on handouts from Washington for your information. If you cherish your freedom, don't leave it all up to BIG GOVERNMENT.

—Barry M. Goldwater

U.S. senator

Jack doesn't belong anymore to just a family. He belongs to the country.

—Joseph P. Kennedy

businessman and diplomat, on his son becoming president

Do you, Ambassador Zorin, deny that the USSR has placed and is placing medium- and intermediate-range missiles and sites in Cuba? Yes or no? Don't wait for the translation. Yes or no? . . . I am prepared to wait for my answer until hell freezes over. And I am also prepared to present the evidence in this room!

—Adlai E. Stevenson

U.S. ambassador to the United Nations

Let every nation know, whether it wishes us well or ill, that we shall pay any price, bear any burden, meet any hardship, support any friend, oppose any foe to assure the survival and the success of liberty.

—John F. Kennedy

thirty-fifth president of the United States

. . . the kind of politician who would cut down a redwood tree, then mount the stump and make a speech for conservation.

—Adlai E. Stevenson

U.S. ambassador to the United Nations, on Richard Nixon

It is impossible, except for theologians, to conceive of a world-wide scandal or a universe-wide scandal; the proof of this is the way people have settled down to living with nuclear fission, radiation poisoning, hydrogen bombs, satellites, and space rockets.

—Mary McCarthy

writer

Finally, to those nations who would make themselves our adversary, we offer not a pledge but a request—that both sides begin anew the quest for peace before the dark powers of destruction unleashed by science engulf all humanity in planned or accidental self-destruction.

—John F. Kennedy

thirty-fifth president of the United States

I feel that this do-or-die, my-country-right-or-wrong kind of patriotism is not merely out of place in a nuclear armed world, it is criminal egotism on a monstrous scale. The world won't be safe until people in all countries recognize it for what it is and, instead of cheering the leader who talks that way, impeach him.

—Dr. Benjamin Spock

activist

Wars of nations are fought to change maps. But wars on poverty are fought to map change.

—Muhammad Ali

boxer

Those who make peaceful revolution impossible will make violent revolution inevitable.

—John F. Kennedy
thirty-fifth president of the United States

All the Way with LBJ

—1964 Democratic campaign slogan (Lyndon B. Johnson)

Khrushchev reminds me of the tiger hunter who has picked a place on the wall to hang the tiger's skin long before he has caught the tiger. This tiger has other ideas.

—John F. Kennedy

thirty-fifth president of the United States

In Your Heart You Know He's Right

—1964 Republican campaign slogan (Barry M. Goldwater)

The United States has to move very fast to even stand still.

—John F. Kennedy

thirty-fifth president of the United States

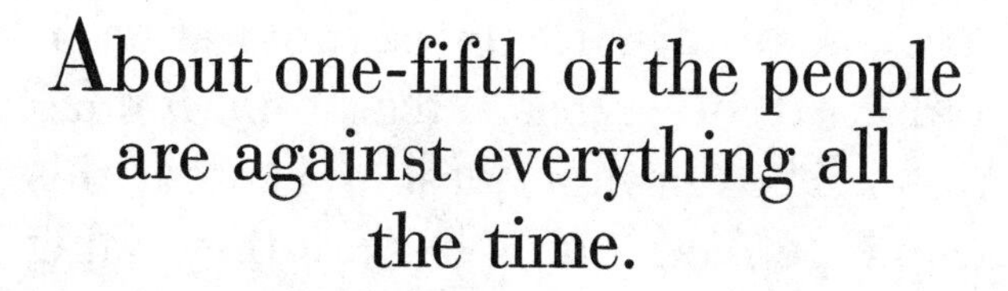

About one-fifth of the people are against everything all the time.

—Robert F. Kennedy
politician

No nation is free from the terrible burdens of historic evils; no nation is composed of angels, free from human frailty. The relevant question is not Is this people perfect? but What are they doing about their imperfections? In what direction are they moving—and how fast?

—Hubert H. Humphrey
vice president of the United States

We will not act prematurely or unnecessarily risk the costs of worldwide nuclear war in which even the fruits of victory would be ashes in our mouth. But neither will we shrink from that risk at any time it must be faced.

—John F. Kennedy

thirty-fifth president of the United States

Lawlessness is lawlessness. Anarchy is anarchy is anarchy. Neither race nor color nor frustration is an excuse for either lawlessness or anarchy.

—Thurgood Marshall

U.S. solicitor general

A Choice Not an Echo

—1964 Republican campaign slogan (Barry M. Goldwater)

When we got into office, the thing that surprised me most was to find that things were just as bad as we'd been saying they were.

—John F. Kennedy

thirty-fifth president of the United States

A president's hardest task is not to do what is right but to know what is right.

—Lyndon B. Johnson

thirty-sixth president of the United States

I have tried to make the whole tone and thrust of this office and this administration one that will demand a higher standard of excellence from every individual.

—John F. Kennedy

thirty-fifth president of the United States

My definition of a free society is a society where it is safe to be unpopular.

—Adlai E. Stevenson

U.S. ambassador to the United Nations

We live in an age of revolution and explosion: exploding bombs, exploding population, revolutionary wars, revolutionary wants. In such an age, we have only two choices, no more. We shall learn to be masters of circumstance, or we shall be its victims.

—Nelson A. Rockefeller
politician

With a good conscience our only sure reward, with history the final judge of our deeds, let us go forth to lead the land we love, asking His blessing and His help, but knowing that here on earth God's work must truly be our own.

—John F. Kennedy

thirty-fifth president of the United States

A nation that represses social problems with police power will become something of an armed camp—which is not a very happy place for either the wardens or the prisoners.

—Michael Harrington

writer

[A] nuclear disaster, spread by winds and waters and fear, could well engulf the great and the small, the rich and the poor, the committed and the uncommitted alike. Mankind must put an end to war or war will put an end to mankind.

—John F. Kennedy

thirty-fifth president of the United States

As it was 189 years ago, so today the cause of America is a revolutionary cause. And I am proud this morning to salute you as fellow revolutionaries. Neither you nor I are willing to accept the tyranny of poverty, nor the dictatorship of ignorance, nor the despotism of ill health, nor the oppression of bias and prejudice and bigotry. We want change. We want progress. We want it both abroad and at home—and we aim to get it.

—Lyndon B. Johnson

thirty-sixth president of the United States

To those people in the huts and villages of half the globe struggling to break the bonds of mass misery, we pledge our best efforts to help them help themselves, for whatever period is required—not because the Communists may be doing it, not because we seek their votes, but because it is right.

—John F. Kennedy

thirty-fifth president of the United States

The hardest job for a politician today is to have the courage to be a moderate. It's easy to take an extreme position.

—Hubert H. Humphrey
vice president of the United States

This nation, this generation, in this hour has man's first chance to build a Great Society, a place where the meaning of man's life matches the marvels of man's labor.

—Lyndon B. Johnson
thirty-sixth president of the United States, accepting Democratic nomination

This is the first time I ever heard it said that the crime is not the burglary, but the discovery of the burglary.

—Adlai E. Stevenson

U.S. ambassador to the United Nations, to Soviet Ambassador Valerian Zorin, who charged that the United States' exposure of nuclear missiles in Cuba threatened peace

This young man—whether he's my son or a stranger—repeatedly declares, "I didn't do it, I didn't do it." And he's shot down. That's not the American way of life. A man is innocent until he's proved guilty.

—Marguerite Oswald

on her son Lee Harvey Oswald, who was killed less than forty-eight hours after the assassination of President John F. Kennedy

He's dead, they've killed him—
oh, Jack, oh, Jack, I love you.

—Jacqueline Kennedy

first lady, en route to the hospital in Dallas

Dear God, please take care of your servant John Fitzgerald Kennedy.

—Jacqueline Kennedy

first lady, inscription for mass cards at her husband's funeral

America is not just a power: it is a promise. It is not enough for our country to be extraordinary in might; it must be exemplary in meaning. Our honor and our role in the world finally depend on the living proof that we are a just society.

—Nelson A. Rockefeller
politician

In the long history of the world, only a few generations have been granted the role of defending freedom in its hour of maximum danger. I do not shrink from this responsibility—I welcome it.

—John F. Kennedy
thirty-fifth president of the United States

Politicians are the same all over. They promise to build bridges, even where there are no rivers.

—Nikita S. Khrushchev

Soviet premier

Nixon's The One

—1968 Republican campaign slogan (Richard M. Nixon)

I know I've got a heart big enough to be president. I know I've got guts enough to be president. But I wonder whether I've got intelligence and ability enough to be president—I wonder if any man does.

—Lyndon B. Johnson

thirty-sixth president of the United States

Our most serious challenges to date have been external—the kind this strong and resourceful country could unite against. While serious external dangers remain, the graver threats today are internal: haphazard urbanization, racial discrimination, disfiguring of the environment, unprecedented interdependence, the dislocation of human identity and motivation created by an affluent society—all resulting in a rising tide of individual and group violence.

—from the final report of the National Commission on the Causes and Prevention of Violence

Rock

I started playing it, and my son said, "Dad, what's that?" I said, "Well, that's God."

—Robert Plant

Led Zeppelin, on playing a Jimi Hendrix best-of collection

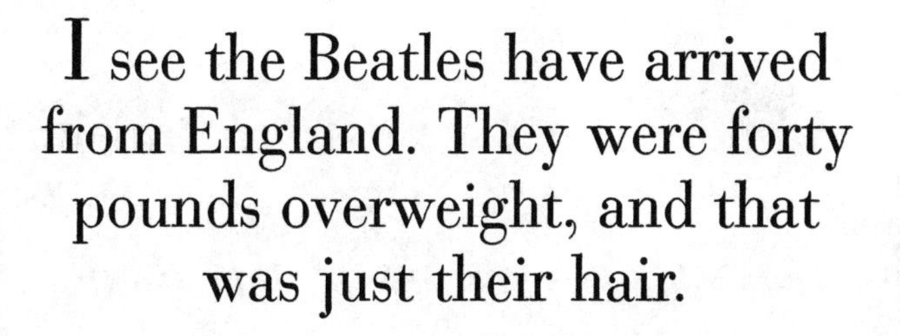

I see the Beatles have arrived from England. They were forty pounds overweight, and that was just their hair.

—Bob Hope

comedian

The Man can't bust our music.

—Columbia Records ad, late 1960s

I knew they'd be bigger than Elvis. I knew they'd be the biggest theatrical attraction in the world.

—Brian Epstein

the Beatles' manager, on the Beatles

I had to come to you behind the Rolling Stones and Beatles.

—Muddy Waters
blues singer and guitarist

I'm the one that's got to die when it's time for me to die, so let me live my life the way I want to.

—Jimi Hendrix

musician/singer

I first heard Hendrix when I was driving my mother's station wagon in New Hampshire. There aren't too many radio stations there—you just got bits and pieces through the static. I heard "Purple Haze," and I thought, "Now we're getting Martian radio."

—Joe Perry

Aerosmith

I wouldn't say we have a publicity strategy for this tour. The Stones, we believe, make their own news.

—David Horowitz

publicist for the 1969 Stones' American tour

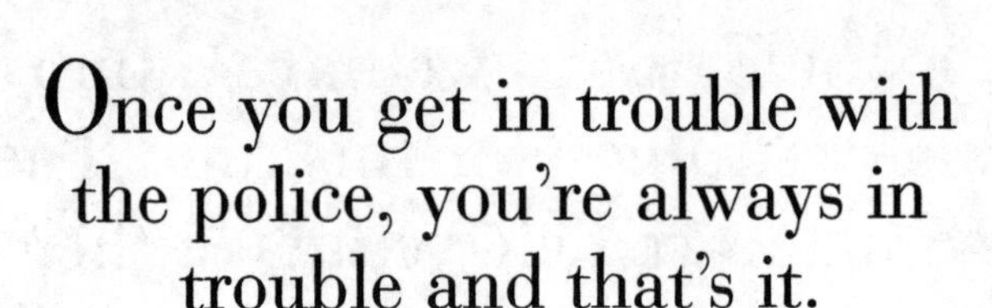

Once you get in trouble with the police, you're always in trouble and that's it.

—Mick Jagger
the Rolling Stones

Bands of the 1960s from San Francisco:

Country Joe and the Fish
Jefferson Airplane
Moby Grape
Great Society
Steve Miller Band
Creedence Clearwater Revival
It's a Beautiful Day
Santana
Hot Tuna
The Grateful Dead
Big Brother and the Holding Company
Tower of Power

Q: Do you think of yourself primarily as a singer or a poet?

A: Oh, I think of myself more as a song and dance man, y'know.

—Bob Dylan

singer/songwriter

Hell no! Everyone is either bald or dead or looks like a plum pudding.

—Joan Baez

singer, on reunion concerts

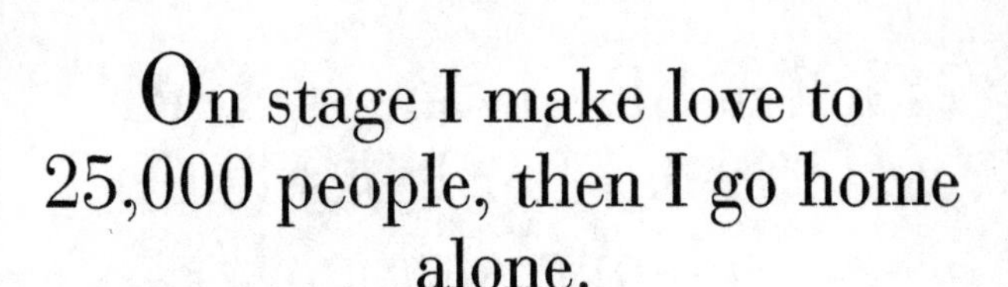

On stage I make love to 25,000 people, then I go home alone.

—Janis Joplin

singer

The Beatles are not merely awful . . . they are so unbelievably horrible, so appallingly unmusical, so dogmatically insensitive to the magic of the art that they qualify as crowned heads of antimusic.

—William F. Buckley, Jr.

writer

I remember calling up *Variety* and accusing the Beatles of stealing my look. The woman there said, "Look, sir, let me tell you something. Their hair is like the Three Stooges, not yours!"

—Tiny Tim
entertainer

Well, to summarize, Big Brother is doing great and I just may be a "star" some day. You know, it's funny. As it gets closer and more probable, being a star is really losing its meaning. But what ever it means I'm ready!

—Janis Joplin

singer, on the band Big Brother and the Holding Company

We're really nervous, but love you all, man, 'cause this is very groovy. Monterey is very groovy. This is something, man. This is our generation, all you people. We're all together. Dig yourselves. It's really groovy.

—Michael Bloomfield

the Electric Flag, at the band's first performance

All my concerts had no sounds in them: they were completely silent. People had to make their own music in their minds.

—Yoko Ono

artist and wife of John Lennon

It was a hot day. I had sandals on, and I kicked them off. Big deal.

—Paul McCartney

the Beatles, responding to why he was pictured barefoot on the cover of the Abbey Road *album and dispelling rumors that it meant he was dead*

Now that I'm here,
where am I?

—Janis Joplin
singer, after making it in New York City

Sometimes I think the only two people who didn't have a good time there was me and the guy that got killed.

—Mick Jagger

the Rolling Stones, on the concert at Altamont, California

In the Top 40, half the songs are *secret* messages to the teen world to drop out, turn on, and groove with the chemicals and light shows at discotheques.

—Art Linkletter

TV personality

The amusing thing about this is its supreme unimportance—after it's all over, and they've outsold everyone else in history, the Monkees will still leave absolutely no mark on American music.

—Crawdaddy! *magazine, on the group's rising fame*

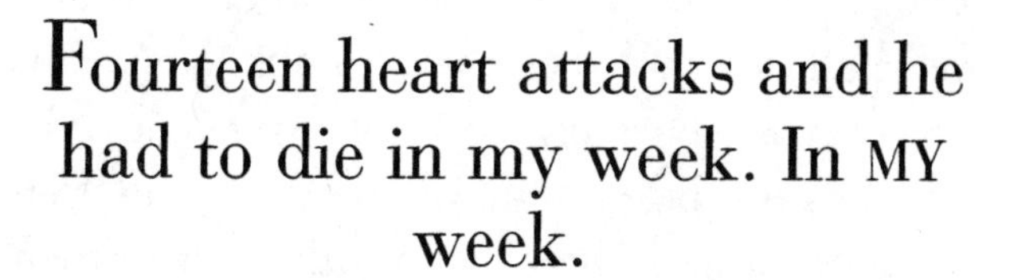

Fourteen heart attacks and he had to die in my week. In MY week.

—Janis Joplin

singer, on the death of President Eisenhower, which prevented her photograph from being on the cover of Newsweek

The name Quicksilver came about because we're all the same astrological sign: Virgo. Gary and Greg are born on the same day. David and I are born on the same day. The four of us were doing our thing. There was a fifth member then, Jimmy Murray, who is a Gemini. Virgos are mercury and mercury is quicksilver and Mercury is a messenger and Virgo is a servant, so Quicksilver Messenger Service.

—John Cipollina
Quicksilver Messenger Service

I'm leaving the group. I want a divorce.

—John Lennon

the Beatles

If you look at pictures from the Woodstock movie and see these people squatting in the mud, you'd say, "What are they going to grow up to be? Just look at these guys!" You know, they turned out to be Wall Street. It just goes to show you the flexibility of the human organism that people who would willingly sit in the mud and chant "no rain" periodically between badly amplified rock groups could suddenly turn out to be the ones to run the U.S. economy.

—Frank Zappa

musician

I thought we stood for infinity.

—Mick Jagger
the Rolling Stones

Greetings and welcome Rolling Stones, our comrades in the desparate [sic] battle against the maniacs who hold power. . . . We will play your music in rock 'n' roll marching bands as we tear down the jails and free the prisoners, as we tear down the State schools and free the students, as we tear down the military bases and arm the poor, as we tattoo BURN BABY BURN! on the bellies of the wardens and generals and create a new society from the ashes of our fires . . . THE ROLLING STONES ARE THAT WHICH SHALL BE! LYNDON JOHNSON—THE YOUTH OF CALIFORNIA DEDICATES ITSELF TO YOUR DESTRUCTION! ROLLING STONES—THE YOUTH OF CALIFORNIA HEARS YOUR MESSAGE! LONG LIVE THE REVOLUTION!!!

—a sign welcoming the Rolling Stones on their first tour of the West Coast

Uh-oh, I think I exposed myself out there . . .

—Jim Morrison

the Doors

I'd rather have ten years of superhypermost than live to be seventy by sitting in some goddamn chair watching TV.

—Janis Joplin

singer

The TV will edit this out, like they'll cut all the groovy things Country Joe said. But I'm gonna say it anyway: John F. Kennedy was shot from a number of different positions by a number of guns. The facts have been suppressed, witnesses killed, and this is your country, ladies and gentlemen.

—David Crosby

the Byrds

I'd rather be dead than singing "Satisfaction" when I'm 45.

—Mick Jagger
the Rolling Stones

Bill Graham was the star of the '60s. He's done more for rock 'n' roll than anyone. More than any of the performers. Because he put on their stages for them. And he opened doors. In the beginning there was great talent, but there were no sound systems. No microphones. Graham came along and changed it. He made the performers a stage. He was what Alan Freed was to the '50s.

—Marty Balin
Jefferson Airplane

I think that for any generation to assert itself as an aware human entity, it has to break with the past, so obviously the kids that are coming along next are not going to have much in common with what we feel. They're going to create their own unique sound.

—Jim Morrison
the Doors

Surrealism had a great effect on me because then I realized that the imagery in my mind wasn't insanity. Surrealism to me is reality.

—John Lennon

the Beatles

I've always wanted to be Brigitte Bardot.

—Bob Dylan
singer/songwriter

Don't do free concerts in America.

—Bill Wyman

the Rolling Stones, on the concert in Altamont, California

Christianity will go. It will vanish and shrink. I needn't argue about that; I'm right and I will be proved right. We're [the Beatles are] more popular than Jesus now; I don't know which will go first—rock 'n' roll or Christianity.

—John Lennon
the Beatles

Remember when you used to watch TV in the '60s and you'd see Perry Como in a cashmere sweater? That's what rock 'n' roll is becoming. It's your parents' music.

—Neil Young

singer

We started out with the Crackers. We tried to call ourselves the Honkies. Everybody kind of backed off from that. It was too . . . straight. So we decided just to call ourselves . . . the Band.

—Richard Manuel

the Band

It was just about what was going on. You know, the punky attitude that had to do with music—hate your mother and stab your father. It's kind of a trend of some sort, and this was a statement that we weren't there. We don't hate our mothers and fathers.

—Robbie Robertson

the Band, referring to a photo of the Band's relatives in the Music from Big Pink *album*

Woodstock

The Woodstock Music and Arts Fair, held in mid-August, 1969, attracted four hundred thousand people who rock 'n' rolled to the sounds of the sixties for three days—rain and shine.

If it all ended tomorrow, we'd be rich and out of work.

—John Lennon

on the Beatles' future

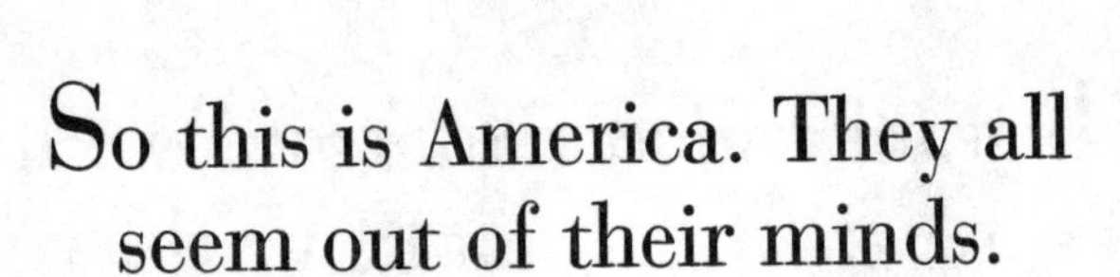

So this is America. They all seem out of their minds.

—Ringo Starr

the Beatles, on arriving in New York for the Beatles' first tour

Back in the late days of the Acid Tests, we were looking for a name. We'd abandoned the Warlocks, it didn't fit any more. One day we were all over at Phil's house smoking DMT. He had a big Oxford dictionary, opened it, and there was "grateful dead," those words juxtaposed. It was one of those moments, y'know, like everything else on the page went blank, diffuse, just sorta oozed away, and there was GRATEFUL DEAD, big black lettered edged all around in gold, man, blasting out at me, such a stunning combination. So I said, "How about Grateful Dead?" and that was it.

—Jerry Garcia
Grateful Dead

Probably the biggest bringdown in my life was being in a pop group and finding out just how much it was like everything it was supposed to be against.

—Mama Cass Elliott

the Mamas and the Papas

If you are a student, a professor, a parent, this is your life because you already know that rock and roll is more than just music; it is the energy center of the new culture and youth revolution.

—Rolling Stone *magazine's ad in the* New York Times

I wouldn't mind dying in a plane crash. It would be a good way to go. I don't want to die of old age or OD or drift off in my sleep. I want to feel what it's like. I want to taste it, hear it, smell it. Death is only going to happen once, right. I don't want to miss it.

—Jim Morrison

the Doors

Commercial rock 'n' roll music is a brutalization of the stream of contemporary Negro church music . . . an obscene looting of a cultural expression.

—Ralph Ellison

writer

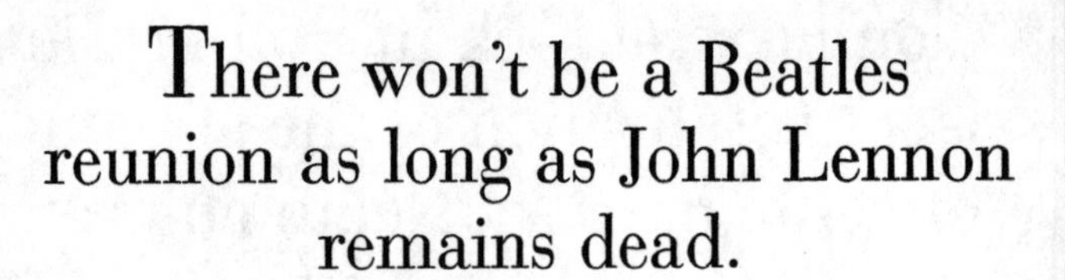

There won't be a Beatles reunion as long as John Lennon remains dead.

—George Harrison
the Beatles

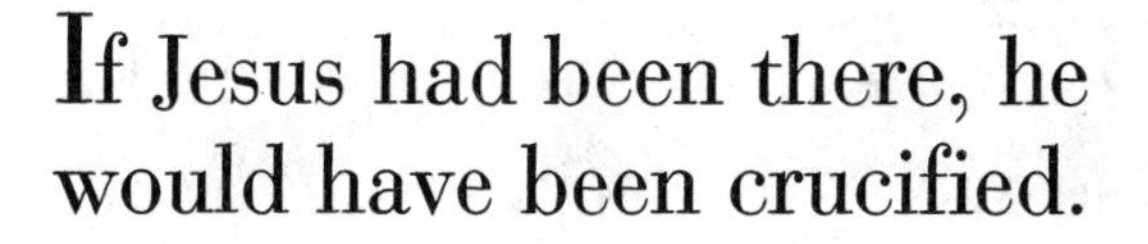

If Jesus had been there, he would have been crucified.

—Mick Jagger

the Rolling Stones, on the concert in Altamont, California

There's three of us in the band so we split everything straight down the middle.

—Mitch Mitchell

the Jimi Hendrix Experience

For the reality of what's happening today in America, we must go to rock 'n' roll, to popular music.

—Ralph J. Gleason
critic

I don't know that. Not very hip on me culture you know.

—John Lennon

the Beatles, when asked by Rolling Stone *magazine for a comment on T. S. Eliot's poem "The Waste Land"*

Q: How does it feel to be the Jesse James of rock?

A: William Bonney would be more accurate. Jesse James was motivated by greed, while Billy the Kid did it for the fun of it. All Americans are outlaws.

—Jim Morrison
the Doors

Security is the only thing I want. Money to do nothing with, money to have in case you wanted to do something.

—Paul McCartney
the Beatles

To me music is always just love, I guess, just happiness. Singin' a happy song. I don't think politics should enter into music. When it does, it makes me a little queasy. 'Cause I don't dig politics that much.

—Marty Balin

Jefferson Airplane

What they thought was an alternative society was basically a field full of six-foot-deep mud laced with LSD.

—Pete Townshend

the Who, on Woodstock

The Vietnam War

We have a habit of trying to get our fingers into every corner of the globe. I think we do that too often, sometimes too heavily, and perhaps a little restraint in the other direction might be beneficial in the years ahead.

—Mike Mansfield
U.S. senator

Our purpose in Vietnam is to prevent the success of aggression. It is not conquest, it is not empire, it is not foreign bases, it is not domination. It is, simply put, just to prevent the forceful conquest of South Vietnam by North Vietnam.

—Lyndon B. Johnson

thirty-sixth president of the United States

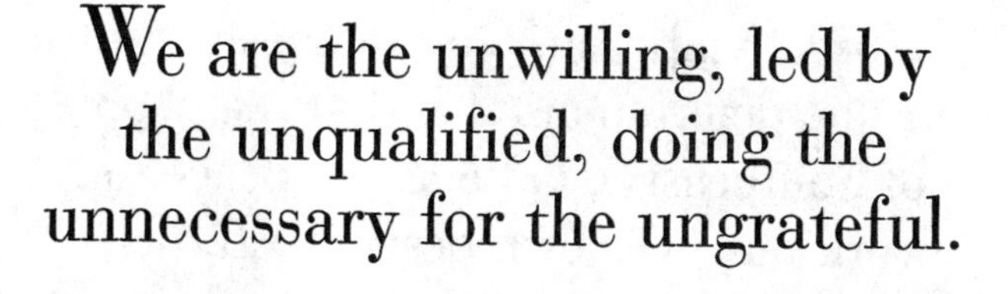

We are the unwilling, led by the unqualified, doing the unnecessary for the ungrateful.

—*graffito*

In that region there is nothing that we covet. There is nothing we seek. There is no territory or no military position or no political ambition. Our one desire and our one determination is that the people of Southeast Asia be left in peace to work out their own destinies in their own ways.

—Lyndon B. Johnson
thirty-sixth president of the United States

—antiwar slogan

Hey, hey, LBJ, how many kids did you kill today?

—*antiwar chant*

Yippies, hippies, yahoos, Black Panthers, lions and tigers alike—I would swap the whole damn zoo for the kind of young Americans I saw in Vietnam.

—Spiro Agnew
vice president of the United States

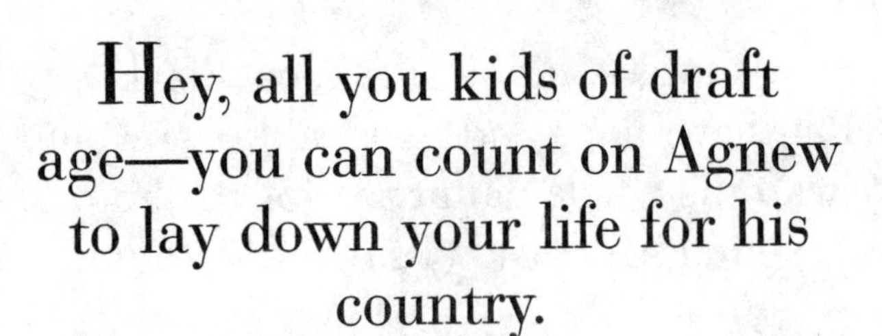

Hey, all you kids of draft age—you can count on Agnew to lay down your life for his country.

—*Anonymous*

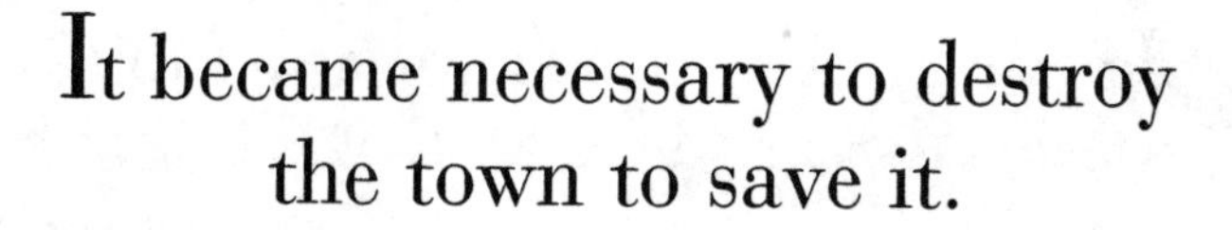

It became necessary to destroy the town to save it.

—an American army major, explaining the decision to bomb and shell Bentre, Vietnam

I wear a suit when I'm arrested. I think it helps to remind people that this isn't a rowdy act but a carefully considered demonstration that I deem worthy of great respect.

—Dr. Benjamin Spock
activist

The corner has definitely been turned toward victory in Vietnam.

—announcement from the Defense Department

—John Lennon and Paul McCartney

the Beatles

Bombing can end the war—
bomb the Pentagon now!

—*graffito*

If any demonstrator ever lays down in front of my car, it'll be the last car he'll ever lay down in front of.

—George C. Wallace
governor of Alabama

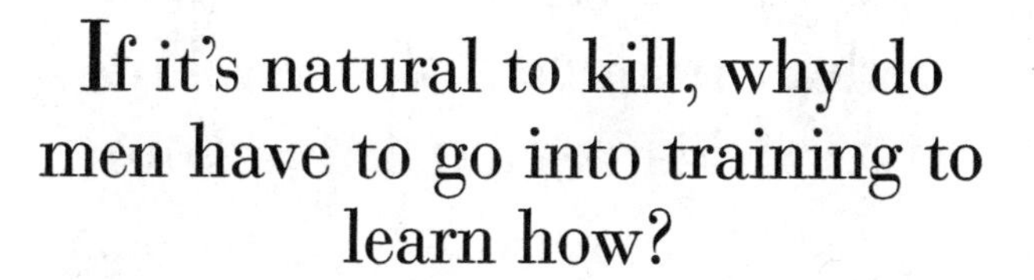

If it's natural to kill, why do men have to go into training to learn how?

—Joan Baez

singer

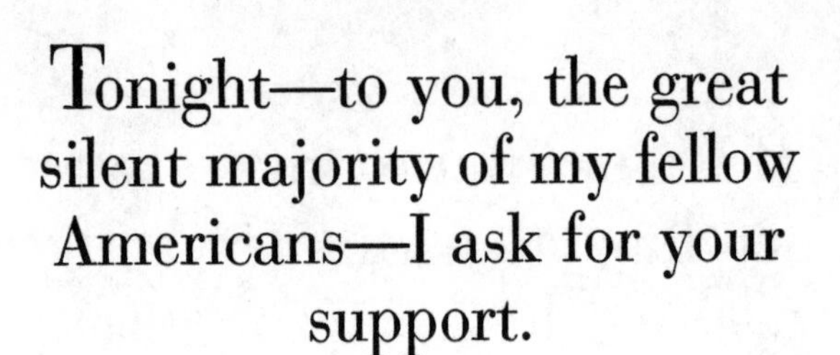

Tonight—to you, the great silent majority of my fellow Americans—I ask for your support.

—Richard M. Nixon

thirty-seventh president of the United States, addressing the nation on his Vietnam War policy

My solution to the problem [of North Vietnam] would be to tell them frankly that they've got to draw in their horns and stop their aggression, or we're going to bomb them back into the Stone Age. And we would shove them back into the Stone Age with Air power or Naval power—not with ground forces.

—General Curtis E. LeMay

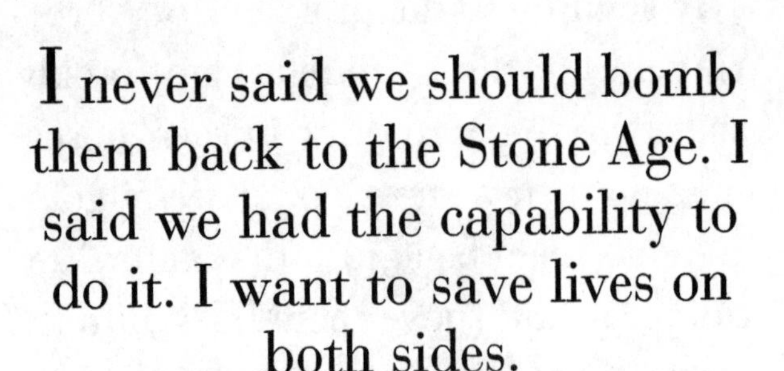

I never said we should bomb them back to the Stone Age. I said we had the capability to do it. I want to save lives on both sides.

—General Curtis E. LeMay
quoted in the Washington Post

The battle against Communism must be joined in Southeast Asia with strength and determination . . . or the United States, inevitably, must surrender the Pacific and take up our defenses on our own shores.

—Lyndon B. Johnson
thirty-sixth president of the United States

I'd rather see America save her soul than her face.

—Norman Thomas

politician

In Asia we face an ambitious and aggressive China, but we have the will and we have the strength to help our Asian friends resist that ambition. Sometimes our folks get a little impatient. Sometimes they rattle their rockets some, and they bluff about their bombs. But we are not about to send American boys 9 or 10,000 miles away from home to do what Asian boys ought to be doing for themselves.

—Lyndon B. Johnson
thirty-sixth president of the United States

We seem bent upon saving the Vietnamese from Ho Chi Minh, even if we have to kill them and demolish their country to do it. . . . I do not intend to remain silent in the face of what I regard as a policy of madness which, sooner or later, will envelop my son and American youth by the millions for years to come.

—George McGovern
politician

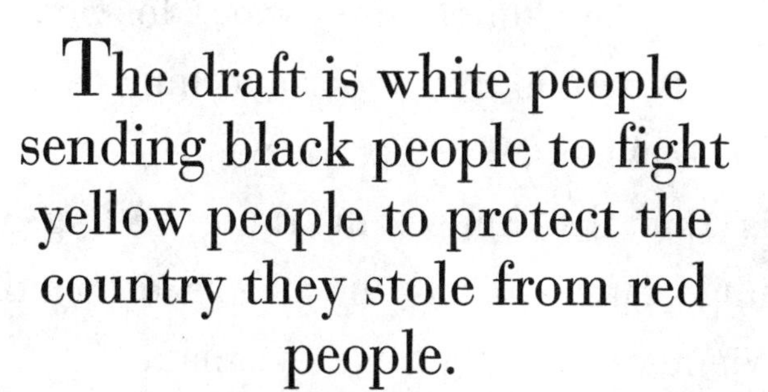

The draft is white people sending black people to fight yellow people to protect the country they stole from red people.

—*from the musical* Hair

by Gerome Ragni and James Rado

What the United States wants for South Vietnam is not the important thing. What North Vietnam wants for South Vietnam is not the important thing. What is important is what the people of South Vietnam want for South Vietnam.

—Richard M. Nixon

thirty-seventh president of the United States

We did not choose to be the guardians of the gate, but there is no one else.

—Lyndon B. Johnson

thirty-sixth president of the United States, on the continued U.S. presence in Vietnam

Make Love,
Not War

—antiwar slogan

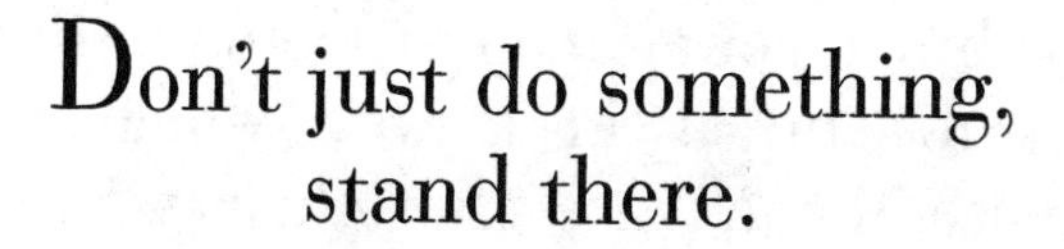

Don't just do something, stand there.

—Daniel Berrigan

activist, advising protesters to think as well as act

I want to end the war to save the lives of those brave young men in Vietnam. But I want to end it in a way which will increase the chance that their younger brothers and their sons will not have to fight in some future Vietnam someplace in the world.

—Richard M. Nixon
thirty-seventh president of the United States

My fellow Americans, we live in an age of anarchy, both abroad and at home.

—Richard M. Nixon

thirty-seventh president of the United States

The only thing that's been a worse flop than the organization of nonviolence has been the organization of violence.

—Joan Baez

singer

We cannot remain silent on Vietnam. We should remember that whatever victory there may be possible, it will have a racial stigma. . . . It will always be the case of a predominantly white power killing an Asian nation. We are interested in peace, not just for Christians but for the whole of humanity.

—Eugene Carson Blake
Protestant minister

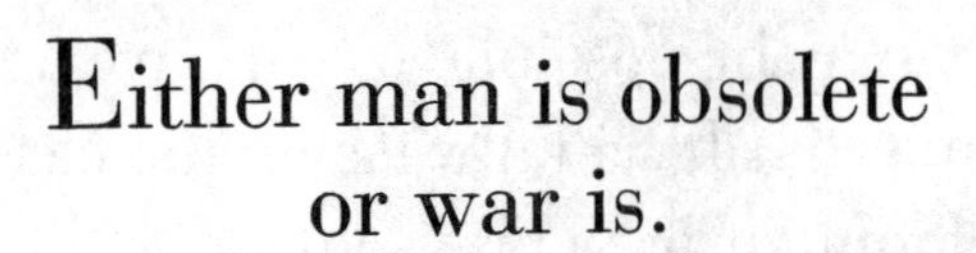

Either man is obsolete
or war is.

—R. Buckminster Fuller

American engineer and inventor

Be kind to cops; they're not cops, they're people in disguise who've been deceived by their own disguise.

—Allen Ginsberg

poet, advice to war protesters

No commander in chief could meet face to face with these soldiers without asking himself: What is it they are doing there? . . . They are there because somewhere, and at some place, the free nations of the world must say again to the militant disciples of Asian communism: This far and no further. The time is now, and the place is Vietnam.

—Lyndon B. Johnson
thirty-sixth president of the United States

What if when they called a war, no one went?

—Abbie Hoffman

activist

You think of those kids out there. I say "kids." I have seen them. They are the greatest. You see these bums, you know, blowing up the campuses. Listen, the boys that are on the college campuses today are the luckiest people in the world, going to the greatest universities, and here they are burning up the books, I mean storming around about this issue—I mean you name it—get rid of the war; there will be another one. Out there we've got kids who are just doing their duty. I have seen them. They stand tall, and they are proud. I am sure they are scared. I was when I was there. But when it really comes down to it, they stand up and, boy, you have to talk up to those men. And they are going to do fine; we've got to stand back of them.

—Richard M. Nixon

thirty-seventh president of the United States

The time has come to stop beating our heads against stone walls under the illusion that we have been appointed policeman to the human race.

—Walter Lippman
journalist

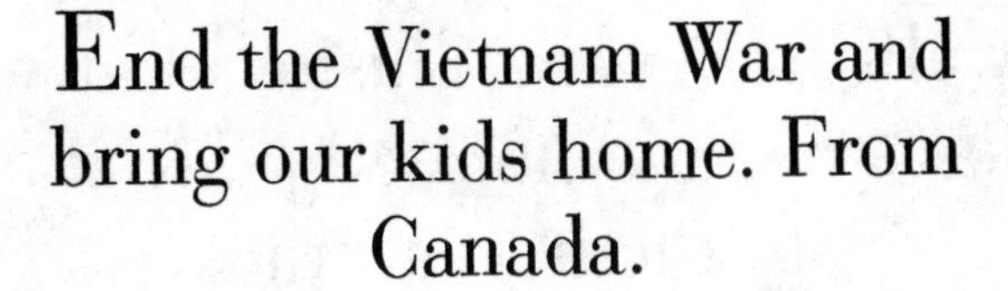

End the Vietnam War and bring our kids home. From Canada.

—*graffito*

Lyndon Johnson came into office seeking a Great Society in America and found instead an ugly little war that consumed him.

—Tom Wicker

author

We met the enemy and he was us.

—attributed to General William C. Westmoreland

Somehow this madness must cease. We must stop now. I speak as a child of God and brother to the suffering poor of Vietnam. I speak for those whose land is being laid waste, whose homes are being destroyed, whose culture is being subverted. I speak for the poor of America who are paying the double price of smashed hopes at home and death and corruption in Vietnam. I speak as a citizen of the world, for the world as it stands aghast at the path we have taken. I speak as an American to the leaders of my own nation. The great initiative in this war is ours. The initiative to stop it must be ours.

—Martin Luther King, Jr.
American clergyman and reformer

The Communist leaders in Moscow, Peking, and Hanoi must fully understand that the United States considers the freedom of South Vietnam vital to our interests. And they must know that we are not bluffing in our determination to defend those interests.

—Gerald R. Ford

U.S. representative

You don't get to choose how you're going to die. Or when. You can only decide how you're going to live. Now.

—Joan Baez

singer

I don't think that unless a greater effort is made by the Government to win popular support that the war can be won out there. In the final analysis, it is their war. They are the ones who have to win it or lose it. We can help them, we can give them equipment, we can send our men out there as advisers, but they have to win it, the people of Vietnam, against the Communists.

—John F. Kennedy
thirty-fifth president of the United States

Vietnam is a military problem. Vietnam is a political problem; and as the war goes on it has become more clearly a moral problem.

—Eugene J. McCarthy

U.S. senator

Declare the United States the winner and begin de-escalation.

—George D. Aiken

U.S. senator

There's a consensus out that it's OK to kill when your government decides who to kill. If you kill inside the country you get in trouble. If you kill outside the country, right time, right season, latest enemy, you get a medal.

—Joan Baez

singer

The doves in this country and some of the media are the cause of fifty-some-odd-thousand Americans being killed and all that money being spent, and all that inflation.

—George C. Wallace

governor of Alabama

But also out here in this dreary, difficult war, I think history will record that this may have been one of America's finest hours, because we took a difficult task and we succeeded.

—Richard M. Nixon

thirty-seventh president of the United States

Some of you have knives, and I ask you to put them up. Some of you may have arms and I ask you to put them up. Get the weapon of nonviolence, the breastplate of righteousness, the armor of truth, and just keep marching.

—Martin Luther King, Jr.

American clergyman and reformer

War is a poor chisel to carve out tomorrows.

—Martin Luther King, Jr.
American clergyman and reformer

. . . we must seek, above all, a world of peace; a world in which peoples dwell together in mutual respect and work together in mutual regard; a world where peace is not a mere interlude between wars, but an incentive to the creative energies of humanity. We will not find such a peace today, or even tomorrow. The obstacles to hope are large and menacing. Yet the goal of a peaceful world must, today and tomorrow, shape our decisions and inspire our purposes.

—John F. Kennedy

thirty-fifth president of the United States

Bombs do not choose. They will hit everything.

—Nikita S. Khrushchev

Soviet premier, at a Moscow rally

Our goal will be peace. Our instrument for achieving peace will be law and justice. Our hope will be that, under these conditions, the vast energies now devoted to weapons of war will instead be used to clothe, house, and feed the entire world. This is the only goal worthy of our aspirations. Competing in this way, nobody will lose, and mankind will gain.

—Richard M. Nixon

thirty-seventh president of the United States

In the councils of government, we must guard against the acquisition of unwarranted influence, whether sought or unsought, by the military-industrial complex.

—Dwight D. Eisenhower

thirty-fourth president of the United States, farewell speech

We are, to put it mildly, in a mess, and there is a strong chance that we shall have exterminated ourselves by the end of the century. Our only consolation will have to be that, as a species, we have had an exciting term of office.

—Desmond Morris

English zoologist and writer

The United States could well declare unilaterally that this stage of the Vietnam War is over—that we have "won" in the sense that our armed forces are in control of most of the field and no potential enemy is in a position to establish its authority over South Vietnam. . . . It may be a far-fetched proposal, but nothing else has worked.

—George D. Aiken

U.S. senator

Victory in Vietnam will not determine who is right, only who is left.

—*graffito*

The bombs in Vietnam explode at home; they destroy the hopes and possibilities for a decent America.

—Martin Luther King, Jr.
American clergyman and reformer

You will kill ten of our men, and we will kill one of yours, and in the end it will be you who tire of it.

—Ho Chi Minh

president of North Vietnam

The war the soldiers tried to stop.

—John F. Kerry

U.S. senator, on how Vietnam would be known to future generations

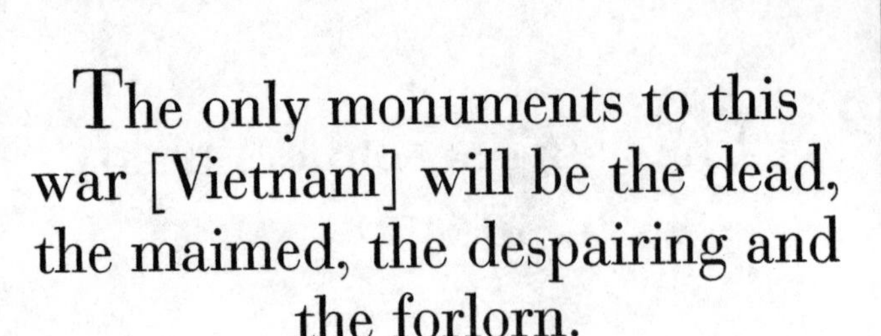

The only monuments to this war [Vietnam] will be the dead, the maimed, the despairing and the forlorn.

—letter from the International Voluntary Services Agency to President Johnson

Counterculture

We Are the People Our Parents Warned Us Against

—slogan of youth movement

Don't shoot.
We are your children.

—Abbie Hoffman

activist, comment to police while protesting outside the Democratic National Convention in August 1968

In this era of affluence and of permissiveness, we have, in all but cultured areas, bred a nation of overprivileged youngsters, saturated with vitamins, television and plastic toys. But they are nurtured from infancy on a Dick-and-Jane literary and artistic level; and the cultural drought, as far as entertainment is concerned, sets in when they are between six and eight.

—Judith Crist
writer

You're either on the bus or off the bus.

—Ken Kesey
novelist

Violence or the threat of violence [must] never be permitted to influence the actions or judgments of the university community. Once it does, the community, almost by definition, ceases to be a university. It is for this reason that from time immemorial expulsion has been the primary instrument of university discipline.

—Richard M. Nixon

thirty-seventh president of the United States

Save Water—Shower With a Friend

—*slogan*

Before I was shot I always suspected I was watching TV instead of living life. Right when I was being shot, I knew I was watching television.

—Andy Warhol

artist, shot in 1968 by Valerie Solanis

Never trust anyone over thirty.

—Abbie Hoffman

activist

They are the most selfish people I know. They just terrify me. They are acting out a society I'd like to live in as an orangutan.

—William Appleman Williams

historian, writer, and educator, on the New Left movement's young adherents

I think a lot of it was puberty.

—Charles C. Marshall III

former member of Students for a Democratic Society, on student rioting

Turn On
Tune In
Drop Out

—slogan

It was a credulous age, perhaps the most credulous ever, and the more rational, the less gullible, the decade claimed to be, the less rational, the more gullible, it showed itself. Never was it easier to gain a reputation as a seer, never was a following so rapidly and readily acquired. Teachers, prophets, sibyls, oracles, mystagogues, avatars, haruspices and mullahs roamed the land, gathering flocks about them as easily as holy men in nineteenth-century Russia, and any philosophy, from Zen Buddhism to macrobiotics and from violence as an end in itself to total inactivity as an end in *it*self, could be sure of a respectful hearing and a group of adherents, however temporary their adherence might prove.

—Bernard Levin

writer

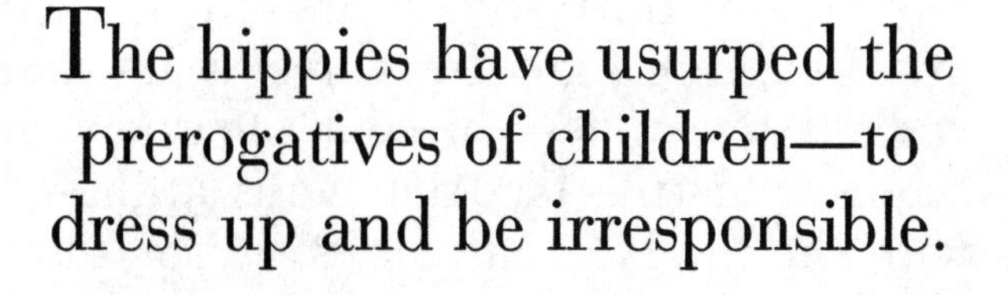

The hippies have usurped the prerogatives of children—to dress up and be irresponsible.

—Anonymous

He's an ideal candidate. He was born in Montana, is thirty-five years old, studied law by candlelight for three years and walked five miles through the snow to school, plus the fact that he is affiliated with the Roman Catholic and Protestant churches, in addition to being a Jew.

—yippie nominating an actual pig for president, summer of 1968

I wouldn't attach too much importance to these student riots. I remember when I was a student at the Sorbonne in Paris, I used to go out and riot occasionally.

—John Foster Dulles

U.S. secretary of state

The first duty of a revolutionary is to get away with it.

—Abbie Hoffman

activist

The lessons of the past are ignored and obliterated in a contemporary antagonism known as the generation gap.

—Spiro Agnew

vice president of the United States

I give the CIA total credit for sponsoring and initiating the entire consciousness movement counterculture events of the 1960s.

—Dr. Timothy Leary
psychologist

For young people today things move so fast there is no problem of adjustment. Before you can adjust to A, B has appeared leading C by the hand, and with D in the distance.

—Louis Kronenberger

writer

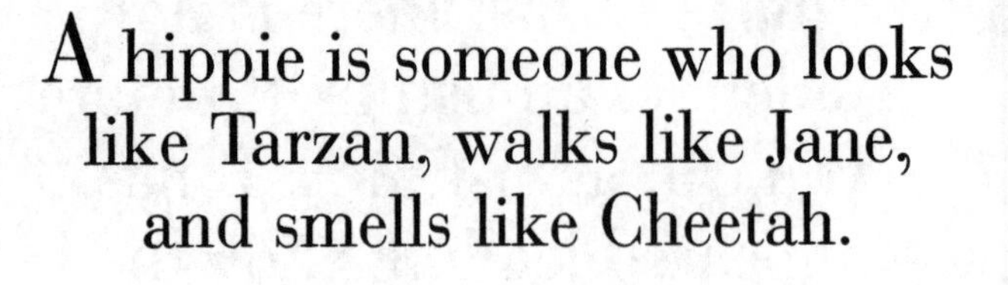

A hippie is someone who looks like Tarzan, walks like Jane, and smells like Cheetah.

—Ronald Reagan

fortieth president of the United States

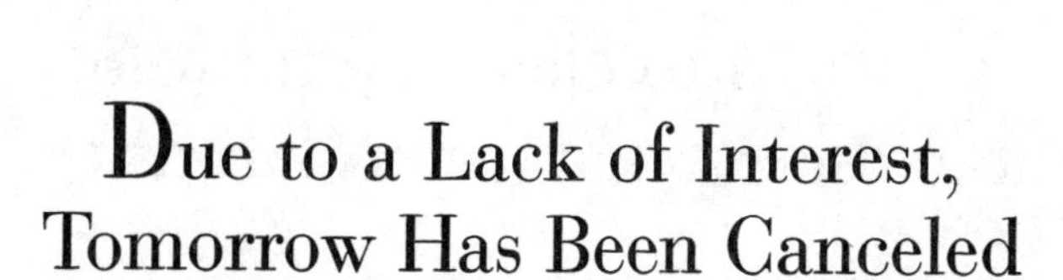

Due to a Lack of Interest, Tomorrow Has Been Canceled

—*slogan*

There's nothing like a week in Chicago to clear the mind of adolescent machismo fantasies.

—Todd Gitlin

ex-president of the Students for a Democratic Society, on the Democratic National Convention in '68

If It Feels Good, Do It

—slogan

They'd go up to a table and tell people, "Hello, I'm your waitress. How's your energy today? Our lunch special is the Gestalt Sushi—we give you a live fish, and you take the responsibility for killing it."

—Robin Williams

comedian

—slogan

Bra-Burners Anonymous

—feminists picketed the 1968 Miss America pageant, throwing constraining pieces of women's underwear in the trash, becoming known to posterity as "bra-burners"

The mass production of distraction is now as much a part of the American way of life as the mass production of automobiles.

—C. Wright Mills

writer

I don't miss the anarchy . . . but I do miss the innocence and the honesty.

—Eldridge Cleaver

former Black Panther, on the sixties

It is not too strong a statement to declare that this is the way civilizations begin to die . . . None of us has the right to suppose it cannot happen here.

—Richard M. Nixon

thirty-seventh president of the United States, on the turmoil on college campuses

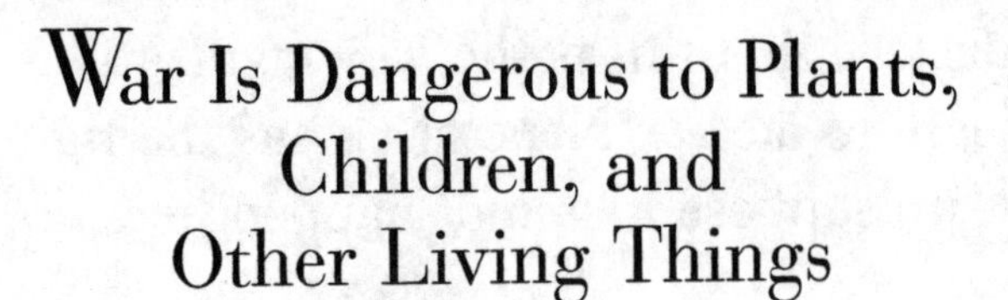

War Is Dangerous to Plants,
Children, and
Other Living Things

—*slogan*

Look, I was made for the sixties. I was enormously happy when I could go to Topanga Canyon, take off all my clothes, and go out and garden. It was nothing if someone came over and you were walking around naked.

—Patti Davis

Ronald Reagan's daughter

My concern today is not with the length of a person's hair but with his conduct.

—Richard M. Nixon

thirty-seventh president of the United States

Arresting them doesn't seem to help because they don't care. . . . It's been my experience that they beat me out of the court back onto the street. I believe that one good crack on the head does more good. If you give them a headache, they go home and usually stay there.

—*anonymous policeman, on the riot at the 1968 Democratic National Convention in Chicago*

You know, we were really poor. Lots of times we had to live on welfare. And you can imagine, we lived in a poor neighborhood, and I had this long hair and wore makeup, and what a scene just to take a walk around the block. Everybody staring—once when I took a walk with my father, a man came up to us and said to my father, "If I had a son like that, I'd take a gun and shoot him."

—Tiny Tim

entertainer, talking with Stephen Schneck

Hippiedom is more than a choice of lifestyle. It's an apolitical systemicide.

—Chuck Hollander

National Student Association

Flower Power

—*slogan*

In almost any society, I think, the quality of the nonconformists is likely to be just as good as and no better than that of the conformists.

—Margaret Mead

American anthropologist

This court will not deny the equal protection of the law to the unwashed, unshod, unkempt, and uninhibited.

—Herman Weinkrantz

judge, ruling on the harassment of hippies

Get Out of Your Mind and Into Your Senses

—*slogan*

Underground Newspapers:

the L.A. Free Press

the Berkeley Barb

the Village Voice

Rolling Stone

The most dangerous thing about student riots is that adults take them seriously.

—Georges Pompidou
president of France

It is rebellion without a cause, rejection without a program, and a refusal of what is, without a vision of what should be.

—Dr. Stanley F. Yolles

director of the National Institute of Mental Health, on alienation as a major cause of drug abuse

Each generation must out of relative obscurity discover its mission, fulfill it, or betray it.

—Frantz Fanon

writer

Civil Rights

I want every American free to stand up for his rights, even if he has to sit down for them.

—John F. Kennedy

thirty-fifth president of the United States

All I was doing was trying to get home from work.

—Rosa Parks

mother of the civil rights movement, on her refusal to move to the back of a bus

Violence is as American as cherry pie.

—H. Rap Brown

civil rights activist

Until justice is blind to color, until education is unaware of race, until opportunity ceases to squint its eyes at pigmentation of human complexions, emancipation will be a proclamation—but it will not be a fact.

—Lyndon B. Johnson

thirty-sixth president of the United States

I just want to do God's will. And he's allowed me to go to the mountain. And I've looked over, and I've seen the promised land! I may not get there with you, but I want you to know tonight that we as a people will get to the promised land.

—Martin Luther King, Jr.

American clergyman and reformer, the night before he was assassinated

You're not supposed to be so blind with patriotism that you can't face reality. Wrong is wrong, no matter who does it or who says it.

—Malcolm X

American religious leader and social activist

I urge you . . . to enact a civil rights law so that we can move forward to eliminate from this country every trace of discrimination and oppression based upon race or color. There could be no greater source of strength to this nation both at home and abroad.

—Lyndon B. Johnson

thirty-sixth president of the United States

Revolutions are never waged singing "We Shall Overcome." Revolutions are based upon bloodshed.

—Malcolm X

American religious leader and social activist

A rioter with a Molotov cocktail in his hands is not fighting for civil rights any more than a Klansman with a sheet on his back and mask on his face. They are both more or less what the law declares them: lawbreakers, destroyers of constitutional rights and liberties, and ultimately destroyers of a free America.

—Lyndon B. Johnson

thirty-sixth president of the United States, on rioting in the Watts section of Los Angeles

The struggle for equal opportunity in America is the struggle for America's soul. The ugliness of bigotry stands in direct contradiction to the very meaning of America.

—Hubert H. Humphrey
vice president of the United States

I miss what we had during that time, a sense of purpose, people coming together, meeting the challenges head-on . . . a kind of solidarity you don't find anymore.

—Myrlie Evers

widow of the slain civil rights activist Medgar Evers

We know the road to freedom has always been stalked by death.

—Angela Davis

American social activist

The core of the civil rights problem is the matter of achieving equal opportunity for Negroes in the labor market. For it stands to reason that all our other civil rights depend on that one for fulfillment. We cannot afford better education for our children, better housing or medical care unless we have jobs.

—Whitney M. Young, Jr.

social worker, educator, and executive director of the National Urban League

He was never mine, totally. He belonged to his people, the struggle, and his country. In a way Medgar constantly prepared me not only to survive but to be able to live and achieve without him.

—Myrlie Evers

widow of the slain civil rights activist

Medgar Evers

The means by which we live have outdistanced the ends for which we live. Our scientific power has outrun our spiritual power. We have guided missiles and misguided men.

—Martin Luther King, Jr.

American clergyman and reformer

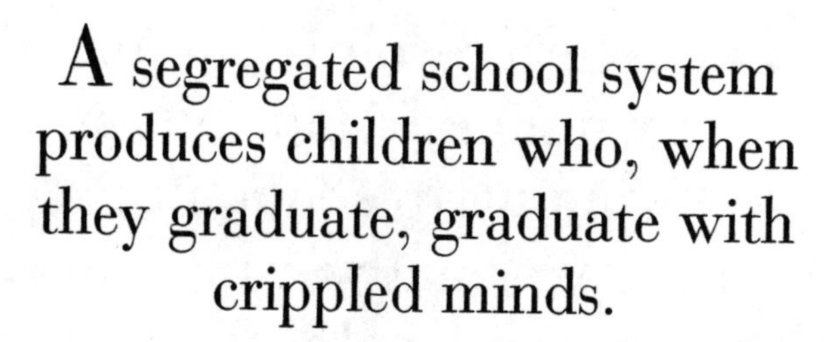

A segregated school system produces children who, when they graduate, graduate with crippled minds.

—Malcolm X

American religious leader and social activist

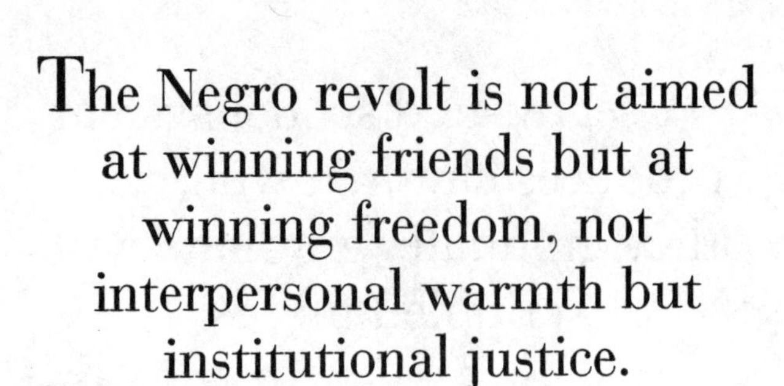

The Negro revolt is not aimed at winning friends but at winning freedom, not interpersonal warmth but institutional justice.

—Harvey G. Cox, Jr.

American theologian, author, and Baptist minister

I have a dream that my four little children will one day live in a nation where they will not be judged by the color of their skin, but by the content of their character.

—Martin Luther King, Jr.

American clergyman and reformer

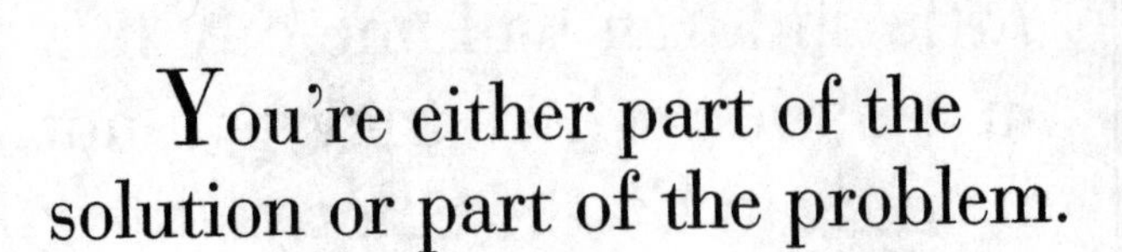

You're either part of the solution or part of the problem.

—attributed to Eldridge Cleaver, writer and activist

In my judgment, the slogan "black power" and what has been associated with it has set the civil rights movement back considerably in the United States over the period of the last several months.

—Robert F. Kennedy

U.S. senator

—*slogan*

Happily for us, students have not tried to overthrow the Government of the United States, but they certainly are making their views felt in public affairs. I think especially of the participation of American students in the great struggle to advance civil and human rights in America. Indeed, even a jail sentence is no longer a dishonor but a proud achievement.

—Adlai E. Stevenson

U.S. ambassador to the United Nations

We shall overcome,
we shall overcome,
We shall overcome some day.
Oh, deep in my heart,
I do believe
We shall overcome some day.

—*song associated with the civil rights movement*

I draw the line in the dust and toss the gauntlet before the feet of tyranny, and I say segregation now, segregation tomorrow, segregation forever.

—George C. Wallace
governor of Alabama

Not actual suffering but the hope of better things incites people to revolt.

—Eric Hoffer

writer

There are those, I know, who will reply that the liberation of humanity, the freedom of man and mind, is nothing but a dream. They are right. It is. It is the American Dream.

—Archibald MacLeish

poet

We will not be satisfied until justice rolls down like waters and righteousness like a mighty stream.

—Martin Luther King, Jr.
American clergyman and reformer

In some cases nonviolence requires more militancy than violence.

—César Chavez

founder of the United Farm Workers

Nonviolence is a powerful and just weapon. . . . which cuts without wounding and ennobles the man who wields it. It is a sword that heals.

—Martin Luther King, Jr.

American clergyman and reformer

Busing is an artificial and inadequate instrument of change which should be abandoned just as soon as we can afford to do so. But we must not take the risk of returning to the kind of segregation, fear, and misunderstanding which produced the very problem in the first place.

—Reubin Askew

lawyer and former governor of Florida

There are no “white” or “colored” signs on the foxholes or graveyards of battle.

—John F. Kennedy
thirty-fifth president of the United States

We must learn to live together as brothers or perish together as fools.

—Martin Luther King, Jr.
American clergyman and reformer

America stands for progress in human rights as well as economic affairs, and a strong America requires the assurance of full and equal rights to all its citizens, of any race, of any color.

—John F. Kennedy

thirty-fifth president of the United States

We have to talk about liberating minds as well as liberating society.

—Angela Davis

American social activist

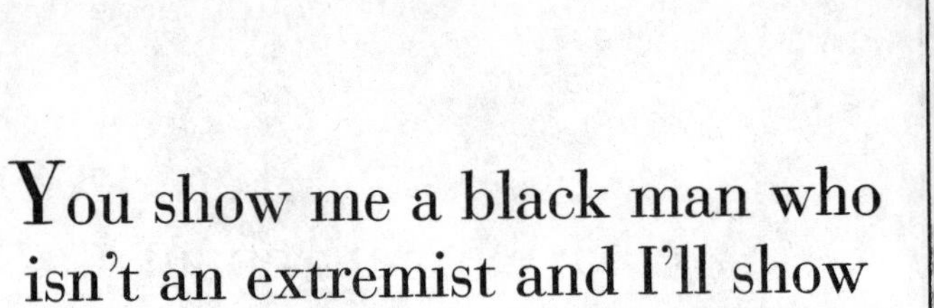

You show me a black man who isn't an extremist and I'll show you one who needs psychiatric attention.

—Malcolm X

American religious leader and social activist

The world has narrowed to a neighborhood before it has broadened to a brotherhood.

—Lyndon B. Johnson

thirty-sixth president of the United States

This nation was founded by men of many nations and backgrounds. It was founded on the principle that all men are created equal, and that the rights of every man are diminished when the rights of one man are threatened.

—John F. Kennedy
thirty-fifth president of the United States

I suggested that we use the panther as our symbol and call our political vehicle the Black Panther Party. The panther is a fierce animal, but he will not attack until he is backed into a corner; then he will strike out.

—Huey Newton

Black Panther Party member

I have a dream that one day every valley shall be exalted, every hill and mountain shall be made low, the rough places will be made straight and the glory of the Lord shall be revealed and all flesh shall see it together.

—Martin Luther King, Jr.

American clergyman and reformer

If violence is wrong in America, violence is wrong abroad. If it is wrong to be violent defending black women and black children and black babies and black men, then it is wrong for America to draft us, and make us violent abroad in defense of her. And if it is right for America to draft us, and teach us how to be violent in defense of her, then it is right for you and me to do whatever is necessary to defend our own people right here in this country.

—Malcolm X

American religious leader and social activist

When this happens, when we let [freedom] ring, we will speed the day when all of God's children, black men and white men, Jews and Gentiles, Protestants and Catholics, will be able to join hands and sing in the words of the old Negro spiritual: "Free at last, free at last, thank God Almighty, we're free at last."

—Martin Luther King, Jr.
American clergyman and reformer

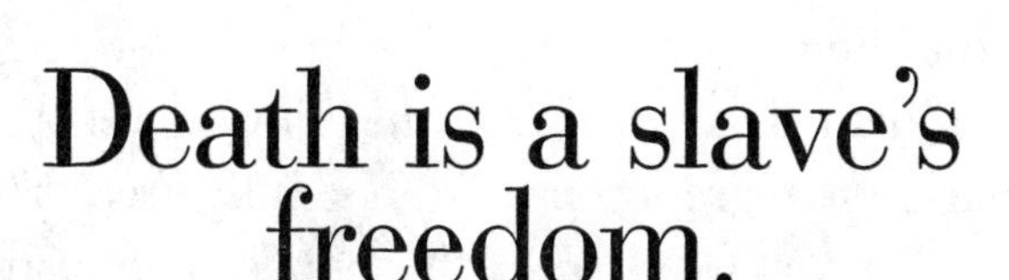

Death is a slave's freedom.

—Nikki Giovanni

American poet, from a speech at the funeral of Martin Luther King, Jr.

One hundred years of delay have passed since President Lincoln freed the slaves, yet their heirs, their grandsons, are not fully free. They are not yet freed from the bonds of injustice; they are not yet freed from social and economic oppression. And this nation, for all its hopes and all its boasts, will not be fully free until all its citizens are free.

—John F. Kennedy

thirty-fifth president of the United States

. . . after you get your freedom, your enemy will respect you.

—Malcolm X

American religious leader and social activist

If we assume that mankind has a right to survive, then we must find an alternative to war and destruction. In our day of space vehicles and guided ballistic missiles, the choice is either nonviolence or nonexistence.

—Martin Luther King, Jr.

American clergyman and reformer

Sometimes, it's [racial prejudice] like a hair across your cheek. You can't see it, you can't find it with your fingers, but you keep brushing at it because the feel of it is irritating.

—Marian Anderson

opera singer

Fashion

The miniskirt enables young ladies to run faster, and because of it, they may have to.

—John V. Lindsay
mayor of New York City

A 17-year-old from North London who called herself Twiggy made looking 17 and starved the fashion image of 1967.

—Axel Madsen

writer

Skirts couldn't get any shorter and remain legal.

—Amy Greene
writer

All women's dresses are merely variations on the eternal struggle between the admitted desire to dress and the unadmitted desire to undress.

—Lin Yutang

educator

Fashions changed, changed again, changed faster and still faster: fashions in politics, in political style, in causes, in music, in popular culture, in myths, in education, in beauty, in heroes and idols, in attitudes, in responses, in work, in love and friendship, in food, in newspapers, in entertainment, in fashion. What had once lasted a generation now lasted a year, what had lasted a year lasted a month, a week, a day.

—Bernard Levin

writer

[It was] much like the Sideburns Fairy, who had been cruising about the city since 1966, visiting young groovies in their sleep and causing them to awake with sideburns running down their jawbones.

—Tom Wolfe

American journalist and novelist

To call a fashion wearable is the kiss of death. No new fashion worth its salt is ever wearable.

—Eugenia Sheppard

journalist

It looks like it's been furnished by discount stores.

—Jacqueline Kennedy
first lady, on the White House

You see, I don't know very much. At school you start history from the caveman, and it takes years to work down all those centuries. I mean, I only went to school until I was 15. So I only got as far as the 17th century.

—Twiggy

model

Ankles are nearly always neat and good-looking, but knees are nearly always not.

—Dwight D. Eisenhower
thirty-fourth president of the United States

Please do not have a fit in the fitting room. Your fashion life begins there.

—Florence Eiseman

children's clothing manufacturer

She changed the White House from a plastic to a crystal bowl.

—Letitia Baldrige

social secretary to Jacqueline Kennedy, on the first lady

Never in the history of fashion has so little material been raised so high to reveal so much that needs to be covered so badly.

— Sir Cecil Beaton

English designer/photographer, on miniskirts

Favorite clothes of the 1960s:

long dresses
jeans
army jackets
beads
headbands
cowboy boots
tie-dyed T-shirts
granny glasses
sandals
go-go boots
bell-bottoms
miniskirts
maxicoats

I do not think it altogether inappropriate to introduce myself. I am the man who accompanied Jacqueline Kennedy to Paris, and I have enjoyed it.

—John F. Kennedy

thirty-fifth president of the United States

By October of 1969 Funky Chic was flying through London like an infected bat, which is to say, silently, blindly, insanely and at night, fangs afoam . . . but with an infallible aim for the main vein.

—Tom Wolfe

American journalist and novelist

Hitched in the '60s:

America's favorite long-legged doll, Barbie, met her match with the production of the "Ken" doll in 1961.

A newspaper reported I spend $30,000 a year buying Paris clothes and that women hate me for it. I couldn't spend that much unless I wore sable underwear.

—Jacqueline Kennedy

first lady

The rush of power to the head is not as becoming as a new hat.

—Helen Van Slyke
American novelist

Legs stay throughout a woman's life.

—Mary Quant

designer, on ageless appeal of miniskirts

Space Exploration

First, I believe that this nation should commit itself to achieving the goal, before this decade is out, of landing a man on the moon and returning him safely to the earth . . . I believe we should go to the moon.

—John F. Kennedy

thirty-fifth president of the United States

Beautiful! Beautiful!
Magnificent desolation.

—Edwin E. ("Buzz") Aldrin, Jr.
U.S. astronaut, on first walk on the moon with Neil A. Armstrong

America is now a space-faring nation . . . a frontier good for millions of years. The only time remotely comparable was when Columbus discovered a whole new world.

—James S. McDonnell

builder of Mercury and Gemini space capsules

To see the earth as we now see it, small and blue and beautiful in that eternal silence where it floats, is to see ourselves as riders on the earth together, brothers on that bright loveliness in the unending night—brothers who *see* now they are truly brothers.

—Archibald MacLeish

poet

Here men from the planet Earth first set foot upon the moon. July 1969 A.D. We came in peace for all mankind.

—plaque planted on the moon by astronauts Neil A. Armstrong and Edwin E. Aldrin Jr.

Problems . . . look mighty small from 150 miles up.

—Roger B. Chaffee

U.S. astronaut, in his last public interview before he died in a fire aboard Apollo 1 during a simulated launch

Because of what you have done the heavens have become a part of man's world, and as you talk to us from the Sea of Tranquillity, it inspires us to redouble our efforts to bring peace and tranquillity to earth.

—Richard M. Nixon

thirty-seventh president of the United States, from earth to Neil Armstrong on the moon

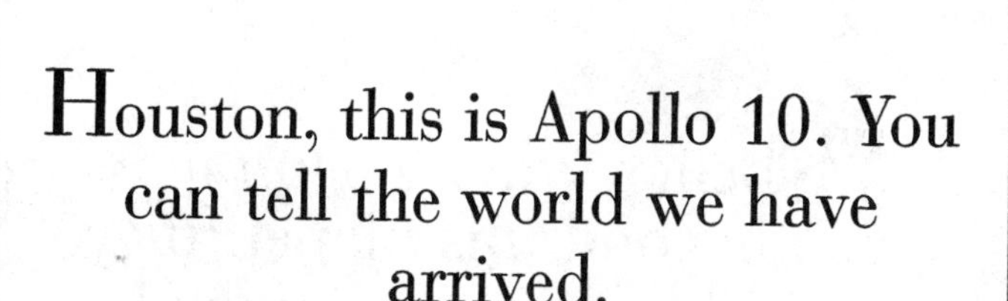

Houston, this is Apollo 10. You can tell the world we have arrived.

—Thomas P. Stafford

U.S. astronaut, from a lunar orbit within nine miles of the moon's surface

We believe that when men reach beyond this planet, they should leave their national differences behind them.

—John F. Kennedy

thirty-fifth president of the United States

It's a vast, lonely, forbidding expanse of nothing . . . rather like clouds and clouds of pumice stone. And it certainly does not appear to be a very inviting place to live or work.

—Frank Borman

U.S. astronaut on Apollo 8, during first manned orbit of the moon, December 25, 1968

This is the greatest week in the history of the world since the Creation.

—Richard M. Nixon

thirty-seventh president of the United States, saluting the crew of the Apollo 11 after the first manned landing on the moon, aboard USS Hornet

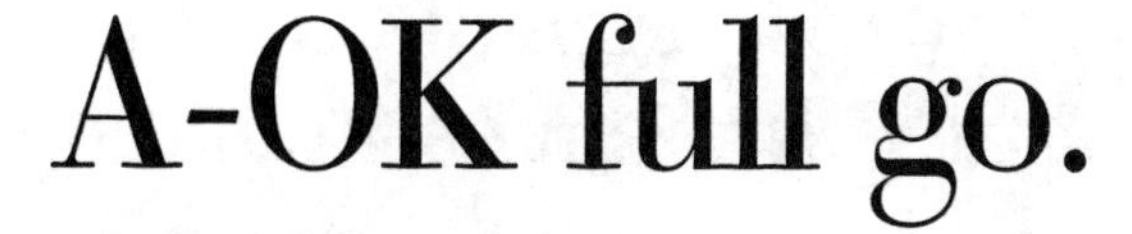

A-OK full go.

—Alan B. Shepard, Jr.

first U.S. astronaut in space, comment at blastoff

In a very real sense, it will not be one man going to the moon . . . it will be an entire nation. For all of us must work to put him there.

—John F. Kennedy

thirty-fifth president of the United States

The emergence of this new world poses a vital issue: will outer space be preserved for peaceful use and developed for the benefit of all mankind? Or will it become another focus for the arms race—and thus an area of dangerous and sterile competition? The choice is urgent. And it is ours to make. The nations of the world have recently united in declaring the continent of Antarctica "off limits" to military preparations. We could extend this principle to an even more important sphere. National vested interests have not yet been developed in space or in celestial bodies. Barriers to agreement are now lower than they will ever be again.

—Dwight D. Eisenhower
thirty-fourth president of the United States

The moon is essentially gray, no color. It looks like plaster of paris, like dirty beach sand with lots of footprints in it.

—James A. Lovell

U.S. astronaut

In orbit now we have a small but harmonious collection of Soviet people.

—Vladimir M. Komarov

Soviet cosmonaut, on the first spaceship to hold three people

Some say God is living there [in space]. I was looking around very attentively, but I did not see anyone there. I did not detect either angels or gods . . . I don't believe in God. I believe in man—his strength, his possibilities, his reason.

—Gherman Titov

Soviet cosmonaut

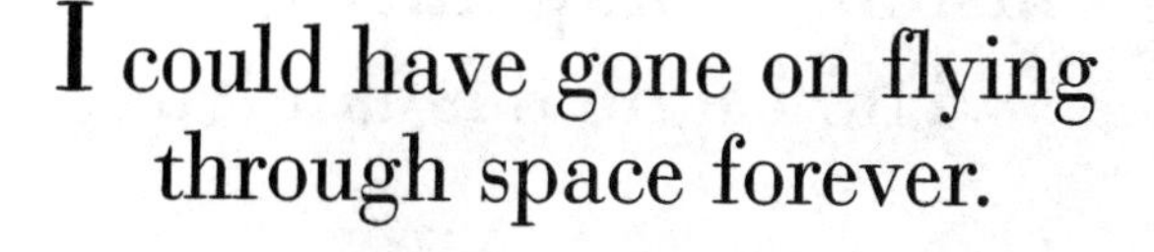

I could have gone on flying through space forever.

—Yuri A. Gagarin

Soviet cosmonaut

Houston, Tranquillity Base here. The Eagle has landed.

—Neil A. Armstrong

astronaut on the Apollo 11 lunar module Eagle, first message to the earth after landing on the moon

This is the first convention of the space age—where a candidate can promise the moon and mean it.

—David Brinkley
TV commentator

That's one small step for man, one giant leap for mankind.

—Neil A. Armstrong

astronaut, on walking on the moon

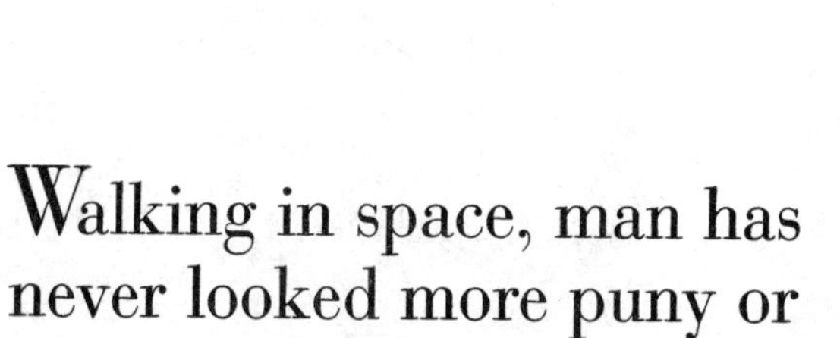

Walking in space, man has never looked more puny or more significant.

—Alexander Chase

writer

We have company tonight.

—Frank Borman

U.S. astronaut, on Gemini 7*'s rendezvous with* Gemini 6 *in space*

It may be, it just may be, that life as we know it with its humanity is more unique than many have thought.

—Lyndon B. Johnson

thirty-sixth president of the United States, on photographs of the planet Mars that revealed a total lack of water, greatly reducing the possibility of the existence of human life there

Many years ago the great British explorer George Mallory, who was to die on Mount Everest, was asked why he wanted to climb it. He said, "Because it is there." Well, space is there, and we're going to climb it, and the moon and the planets are there, and new hopes for knowledge and peace are there.

—John F. Kennedy

thirty-fifth president of the United States

A Miscellany

I have never quite understood this sex symbol business, but if I'm going to be a symbol of something, I'd rather have it sex than some of the other things they've got symbols for.

—Marilyn Monroe

actress

Reel Talk:

'Twas the night before Christmas and all through the house, not a creature was stirrin'. Nothing'. No action. Dullsville. You married?

—Hope Holiday

in The Apartment *(1960)*

We are all refugees of a future that never happened.

—Lee Weiner

activist

Reel Talk:

Mrs. Robinson, you're trying to seduce me. Aren't you?

—Dustin Hoffman

to Anne Bancroft in The Graduate *(1967)*

The only trouble with sexually liberated women is that there aren't enough sexually liberated men to go around.

—Gloria Steinem

writer and activist for women's rights

Reel Talk:

Patricia Neal: I was married to Ed for six years. The only thing he was ever good for was to scratch my back where I couldn't reach it.

Paul Newman: You still got that itch?

—Hud *(1963)*

We have produced a world of contented bodies and discontented minds.

—Adam Clayton Powell, Jr.

political and religious leader

John Clellon Holmes . . . and I were sitting around trying to think up the meaning of the Lost Generation and the subsequent Existentialism and I said, "You know, this is really a beat generation" and he leapt up and said "That's it, that's right!"

—Jack Kerouac

novelist and spokesperson for the Beat generation of the 1950s and '60s

Reel Talk:

First we'll have an orgy, and then we'll go see Tony Bennett.

—Elliott Gould

in Bob & Carol & Ted & Alice *(1969)*

One has the uneasy feeling that he is always on the verge of pronouncing himself the victim of some clandestine plot.

—Arthur Schlesinger

historian, on Richard M. Nixon

I have one word for you,
Benjamin—plastics.

—Walter Brooke
to Dustin Hoffman in
The Graduate *(1967)*

Pop Artists:

Robert Indiana

Jasper Johns

Roy Lichtenstein

Claes Oldenburg

Larry Rivers

Andy Warhol

Reel Talk:

You look pretty good without your shirt on, you know. The sight of that through the kitchen window made me put down my dishtowel more ’n once.

—Patricia Neal

to Paul Newman in Hud *(1963)*

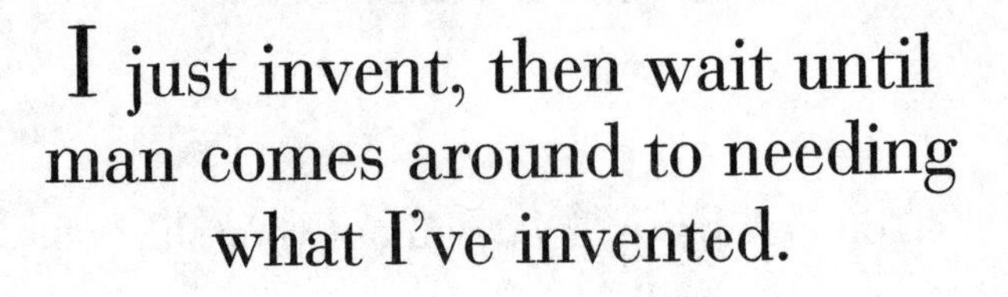
I just invent, then wait until man comes around to needing what I've invented.

—R. Buckminster Fuller

American engineer and inventor

Reel Talk:

Nobody laughs at me because I laugh first. At me. Me from Seattle. Me with no education. Me with no talent, as you kept reminding me my whole life. Well, Mama, look at me now. I'm a star. Look. Look how I live. Look at my friends. Look where I'm going. I'm not staying in burlesque. I'm moving—maybe up, maybe down—but wherever it is, I'm enjoying it. I'm having the time of my life because, for the first time, it *is* my life. And I love it. I love every second of it.

—Natalie Wood
to Rosalind Russell in Gypsy *(1962)*

Popular Expressions:

Can you dig it?

Oh wow

Right on!

Out of sight

Far out

Peace

What's happenin'?

Let it all hang out!

Bummer!

Groovy!

Freak out!

Good vibes!

Where it's at

To put it bluntly, I seem to be a whole superstructure with no foundation. But I'm working on the foundation.

—Marilyn Monroe

actress

Reel Talk:

Always remember two things: I love you—and the name of the bank.

—Debbie Reynolds
in The Unsinkable Molly Brown *(1964)*

Perfection itself is imperfection.

—Vladimir Horowitz

concert pianist

Reel Talk:

In case you think I'm a fast worker, I've never told a woman I loved her or signed "Love" to a letter except to my folks. And I'm over thirty years old. Naturally, now that something's hit me, I can't waste any time.

—James Broderick
in The Group *(1966)*

I Am a Student. Please Do Not Fold, Spindle, or Mutilate Me.

—slogan

New music: new listening. Not an attempt to understand something that is being said, for, if something were being said, the sounds would be given the shapes of words. Just an attention to the activity of sounds.

—John Cage
composer

Reel Talk:

All you have to do is give up a little bit of you for him. Don't make everything a game—just late at night in that little room upstairs. Take care of him. Make him feel important. If you can do that, you'll have a happy and wonderful marriage—like two out of every ten couples.

—Mildred Natwick

to Jane Fonda in Barefoot in the Park *(1967)*

In the future everyone will be famous for fifteen minutes.

—Andy Warhol
artist

Reel Talk:

Who said anything about getting married? I feel that way about my girl because she *is* my girl. You'd never catch me feeling that way about a wife. Look Harvey, I've got a perfect setup. Why spoil it by getting married?

—Walter Matthau

in Cactus Flower *(1969)*

A spirit of national masochism prevails, encouraged by an effete corps of impudent snobs who characterize themselves as intellectuals.

—Spiro Agnew

vice president of the United States

My husband runs what is called an educational television network. You must have seen some of the wonderful work they put on. Who else gives you a close look at gum surgery? Just as you're sitting down to dinner?

—Chris Chase

writer

Reel Talk:

I swear, if you existed I'd divorce you.

—Elizabeth Taylor

to Richard Burton in Who's Afraid of Virginia Woolf? *(1966)*

The problem that has no name—which is simply the fact that American women are kept from growing to their full human capacities—is taking a far greater toll on the physical and mental health of our country than any known disease.

—Betty Friedan

writer and feminist

Dig. The only honest art form is laughter, comedy. You can't fake it, Jim. Try to fake three laughs in an hour—ha ha ha ha ha—they'll take you away, man. You can't.

—Lenny Bruce

comedian

Reel Talk:

Laurence Harvey: Look, Gloria, I have to spend at least tonight with [my wife].

Elizabeth Taylor: A good night's sleep will be the best thing for you.

—Butterfield 8 *(1960)*

It wasn't suicide. It wasn't sleeping pills, it wasn't cirrhosis. I think she was just tired, like a flower that blooms and gives joy and beauty to the world and then wilts away.

—Liza Minnelli

singer/actress, on the death of her mother, Judy Garland

Reel Talk:

Fred MacMurray: You see a girl a couple of times a week, just for laughs, and right away they think you're going to divorce your wife. Now I ask you, is that fair?

Jack Lemmon: No sir, it's very unfair—especially to your wife.

—The Apartment *(1960)*

I always wished I had died, and I still wish that, because I could have gotten the whole thing over with.

—Andy Warhol

artist, on being seriously wounded in 1968

Reel Talk:

Peter O'Toole: Give me a little peace.
Katharine Hepburn: A little? Why so modest? How about eternal peace?

—The Lion in Winter *(1968)*

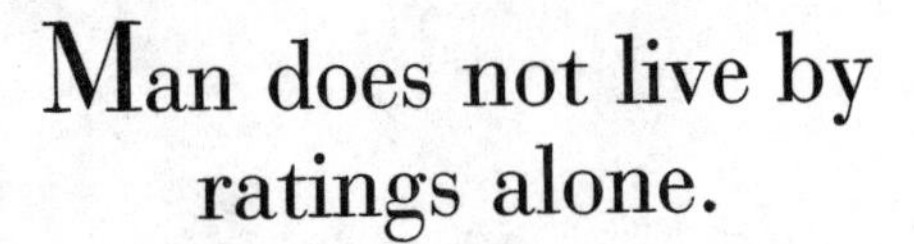

Man does not live by ratings alone.

—Newton Minow

Federal Communications Commission

Reel Talk:

What we've got here is a failure to communicate.

—Strother Martin
in Cool Hand Luke *(1967)*

I am for an art that is political-erotical-mystical, that does something other than sit on its ass in a museum.

—Claes Oldenburg

artist

Reel Talk:

Your idea of fidelity is not having more than one man in the bed at the same time.

—Dirk Bogarde

to Julie Christie in Darling *(1965)*

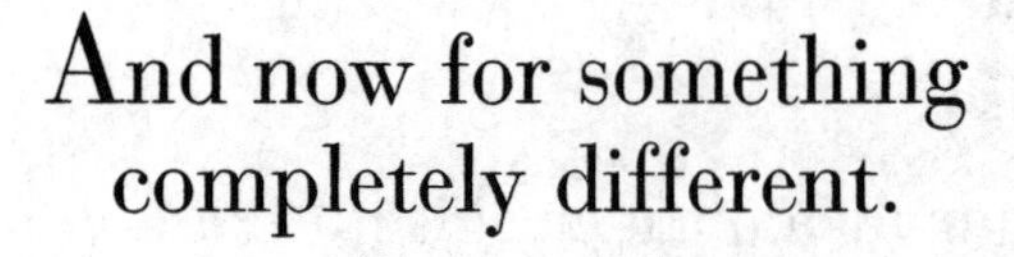

And now for something completely different.

—*catchphrase from* Monty Python's Flying Circus

I invite you to sit down in front of your television set when your station goes on the air and stay there without a book, magazine, newspaper, profit-and-loss sheet, or rating book to distract you—and keep your eyes glued to that set until the station signs off. I can assure you that you will observe a vast wasteland.

—Newton Minow

Federal Communications Commission, from a speech at the National Association of Broadcasters

Reel Talk:

Sing out, Louise. Sing out!

—Rosalind Russell
in Gypsy *(1962)*

Not only do I knock ’em out, I pick the round.

—Muhammad Ali

boxer

Television is business, and business is America.

—Bill Cosby

actor

I am a deeply superficial person.

—Andy Warhol
artist

It was hard to get a painting that was despicable enough so that no one would hang it. . . . The one thing everyone hated was commercial art; apparently they didn't hate that enough either.

—Roy Lichtenstein

artist

Reel Talk:

Look, with these gals that want to buy it, most of 'em are old and dignified—social-register types, you know what I mean? They can't be trottin' down to Times Square to pick out the merchandise.

—Dustin Hoffman

in Midnight Cowboy *(1969)*

Is it larger than a bread box?

—*favorite question for guests on the TV show* "What's My Line?"

We must never forget that art is not a form of propaganda; it is a form of truth.

—John F. Kennedy
thirty-fifth president of the United States

Reel Talk:

Suddenly, you're afraid, and you don't know what you're afraid of. Did you ever get that feeling? . . . Well, when I get it, the only thing that does any good is to jump into a cab and go to Tiffany's. Calms me down right away. The quietness and the proud look of it. Nothing very bad could happen to you there.

—Audrey Hepburn
in Breakfast at Tiffany's *(1961)*

The feminine mystique has succeeded in burying millions of American women alive.

—Betty Friedan

author of The Feminine Mystique *(1963)*

We want and deserve tin-can architecture in a tin-horn culture. And we will probably be judged not by the monuments we build but by those we have destroyed.

—New York Times

on 1963 demolition of Pennsylvania Station

Reel Talk:

Believe you me, if it didn't take men to make babies, I wouldn't have anything to do with any of you!

—Gena Rowlands

to Kirk Douglas in Lonely Are the Brave *(1962)*

Float like a butterfly,
Sting like a bee!

—Muhammad Ali

boxer, on his boxing style

Senator McCarthy and television came into prominence together, and it is a nice irony that a medium so perfectly made to order for a demagogue should have proved to be the means of his undoing, thanks as much to [Edward R.] Murrow and [Fred] Friendly as to the Senator's own extraordinary capers.

—Gore Vidal

writer

Reel Talk:

Queen Cleopatra is widely read, well versed in the natural sciences and mathematics. She speaks seven languages proficiently. Were she not a woman, one would consider her to be an intellectual.

—Andrew Keir

about Elizabeth Taylor in Cleopatra *(1963)*

Each suburban wife struggled with it alone. As she made the beds, shopped for groceries, matched slipcover material, ate peanut butter sandwiches with her children, chauffeured Cub Scouts and Brownies, lay beside her husband at night—she was afraid to ask even of herself the silent question—"Is this all?"

—Betty Friedan

author of The Feminine Mystique *(1963)*

Reel Talk:

Martha? Rubbing alcohol for you?

—Richard Burton to Elizabeth Taylor in *Who's Afraid of Virginia Woolf?* (1966)

I am a jelly doughnut.
("Ich bin ein Berliner.")

—John F. Kennedy, thirty-fifth president of the United States, speaking in Germany (Kennedy meant to say "I am a citizen of Berlin," but his shaky German changed the meaning of his words entirely.)

Reel Talk:

She's like catnip to every cat in town.

—Tom Ahearne (bartender)
about Elizabeth Taylor in *Butterfield 8* (1960)

The steady pressure to consume, absorb, participate, receive, by eye, ear, mouth, and mail involves a cruelty to intestines, blood pressure, and psyche unparalleled in history. We are being killed with kindness. We are being stifled with cultural and material joys.

—Herbert Gold

writer

The art of our era is not art, but technology. Today Rembrandt is painting automobiles; Shakespeare is writing research reports; Michelangelo is designing more efficient bank lobbies.

—Howard Sparks
writer

The Medium Is the Message.

—Marshall McLuhan

communications theorist

This book was typeset in
Adobe Bauer Bodoni.

Book design and typesetting by
Judith Stagnitto Abbate

Cover design by Sara Stemen